Night's Pardons

Night's Pardons
by James Sallis

Five Oaks Press
FIVE-OAKS-PRESS.COM

Copyright © 2016 James Sallis
All rights reserved. First edition
Printed in the United States of America

ISBN: 978-1-944355-08-1

Five Oaks Press
Newburgh, NY 12550
five-oaks-press.com
editor@five-oaks-press.com

Cover Art: "After Dinner Speaker" by Philip C. Curtis, is reproduced by generous permission of The Philip C. Curtis Charitable Trust for the Encouragement of Art, Philip J. Curtis and Janie Ellis, Trustees.

Acknowledgments

Individual poems first appeared, often in somewhat different form, in *The 2River View*, *Mudlark*, *Melic Review*, the author's collection *A Few Last Words*, *Gloss*, *Epiphany*, *Grasslimb*, *3 AM*, *Mickle Street Review*, *Quark*, *The James Sallis Reader*, *In Posse Review*, *The Coe Review*, *Open Places* and *Moonshine Baby*. Many appear here for the first time.

Contents

I.

Thwack-Thwack	7
Texting My Left Brain	8
Two Deserts	9
Me and My Drone	10
Ringtone	11
At Night	12
Kong	13
Confession	14
Down With the Undead	15
Passion	16
Amazing Tales of Super Science	17

II.

Book of Hours	21
What the Days Bring	22
Late News	23
Watching the Clock	24
Sheridan Square	25
June 6th	27
Return	28
In May	29

III.

The Sisters of Sheldon Street	33
Spy Story	34
Of the Voyage	35
Speechless	36
Victory	37
Saviors	38
Gauge	39
Stand-Up	41
Badges	42
Water	43
Artaud	44
For Queneau	45
New Life	46

Scat Singers	47
Ars Poetica	48
Stalking the Wild MFA	49
Screen Doors	50
Baroque	51

IV. New Surrealist Poems

The Surrealist Comes to Black Rock	55
The Surrealist Travels by Train	56
The Girl the Surrealist Left Behind	57
The Surrealist Relocates	58
The Plan Behind Improvisation	59
Surrealist Bird	60
The Surrealist Prays	61
Surrealist on the Move	62
The Surrealist Remembers His Friend	63

V.

Done	67
Loss	68
Seasons	69
Family	70
Fall	71
Some Propositions	72
Final Landscape	73
Christmas 1969	74

VI.

Compass	79
Last Call	80
Once Upon Again	81
The Surrealist Is Interviewed on 60 Minutes	82
Lost Letters	83
When I Had the Sky	84
As We Were	85
Resolve	86
Fortune	87

To Linda

"What key?"

I

Thwack-Thwack

You're dredged from sleep
by the sound of helicopters.

Their lights slice through your blinds,
cross floor and wall
like thoughts you can't quite get hold of,
and are gone.

You think of all those movies:
ominous shadows, the man barely hanging on,
extractions, last-minute saves.
Of your uncle who died in Vietnam.

You think you hear
the crackle of police radios just outside.
You turn in bed
to your wife or husband, who is not there.

Texting My Left Brain

You do so often disapprove. I could tell
by how my hand on Friday
hesitated
on the way to its prize, how last Tuesday
that swift movement in the room's corner
so quickly became nothing.

Truly I thought the light
slanting in through blinds,
how it touched shyly here, boldly there,
crabbing its way across the table top,
would explain everything.

Then you arrived
to set the room in order.

Lamps came on, walls and corners
remembered one another. Proudly
the window put on display
the reasonable fact of sky and tree.

Two Deserts

    (for a returning soldier)

When I came home, home to you I thought, I brought
so many bodies
with me.

They weighed nothing. Didn't speak or ask much
or pass judgment. Even in crowds
I was never alone.

None of them had faces, of course, not
any longer.

When lights came on, I could hear the scamper
of them inside me, fleeing.

When you were a child, every night,
you dreamed of bears.
The bears have not forgotten you.

Me and My Drone

Thank you Daddy
Because I'm safe now

I was 8 when you built it
Because I was afraid

You thought it was for show only
Because belief was enough
I believed

It took out two kids on the playground
That first time
Because they picked on me

Thank you Daddy

Because I was small for my age
An easy target

The city's so quiet now
Never lonely though
I have my drone

Ringtone

The phone rings and I don't answer.
Someone else has died.

Thursday my friend called
to tell me he was next, he could feel it
in his bones, the black-rimmed letter
was about to be delivered.

But morning brings another sun.
New apples clear their throats
and drop to the ground. The hive of bees
that has moved into the wall
between my neighbor's home and mine
hums with expectation.

At Night

Heads down, torch blinking
Along the sand, we follow. Here the tracks
Of feet, disparallel lines
Sliding away and back on either side,
As on polygraphs. The batteries are old,
Dimming. Our breath and the fog
Gather towards the torch. And there, beside, behind,
The mark of something else, something like
Limp, trailing wings.

Ahead in the darkness
There is a click, almost unheard, as of
Chambers revolving to the next full load,
Beetles closing wings
Into coffinlike cases. The torch stammers,
Flashes. Flares. Dies.
In your hand now, it is itself
Something else.

Kong

Unaccustomed, unknowing, the intruders believe
this celebration
to be for a marriage of some gnarly sort,

or a sly priest's con
to get the blond into bed or whatever serves as such,

but it's for you.

The intruders bring shoes, toothbrushes,
flowers pressed into books, sweat socks,
bright metal chains on their necks. This gift,
they say, of civilization.

Don't believe them, Great Beast, don't
come out to play. Look to your left:
one channel up, the world is being saved
by a twelve-year-old the size of your fist.

Confession

I make no bones of it:
She was a werewolf, and I loved her.

We all know: Hard enough, always,
to give oneself over.

At her paws and teats I learned:
Civilization is not a stain that wildness
overcomes. They are one and the same.

Her coat was damp when we first met.
She limped. We had both been hurt.
I was cold. Her hot breath warmed me.

Could it last? Of course not.
We knew that. That went unsaid

as in the bowels of vast Chicago
that single winter we dwelled in a world
far away from Dr. Phil,

from events of the day, from
all the angers that pass as wisdom.

Down With the Undead

This part is true:
I loved every bit of flesh
that fell from her.

This is all you need to know.
None of the rest of your questions
matter,

nor will I suggest again
how filled the world is with things
to which *you* do not matter.

Our cave looms up behind me
like a hole punched through
to the black.

Out at world's edge I see
the rot begin as bits start to fall away,
bits that once I loved.

Passion

1.

Asking forgiveness
alone, I appear
before you.

Favor nor love
do I expect, nor
explanation.

Speak the sentence.

2.

You are becoming
your animal tonight, your totem:
wildness in the eyes,
one leg restless, twitching,
as you dream.

Deep within
the mists of that dream
villagers march crookedly
uphill to the castle,
and blood flows down.

3.

The angels all come
at the same time. They
have been to a movie,
a thriller, and are still talking
about it, still wearing
their 3-D glasses. Bits of popcorn
cling to their robes. They
eat up everything in the house,
but drink only water.

Amazing Tales of Super Science

Terror of the ordinary.
It strikes unannounced: the potato
leaping from its bin, bland eyes ablaze,
the orange opening itself with the sound
of wet sneakers coming towards you,
windows opaque with rain
or misunderstanding.

***

It was in the first August, on a warm cloudy day, that Grumbly invented space. We must have something to hold all the things of the world apart, he said. Experimenting first with a variety of small wedges, then with sandbags from which gradually, grain by grain, he extracted sand, he returned apace to the wedges, over several months increasing their sizes incrementally until at last, when he removed his wedges, the things of the world stood alone.

***

After the pigs have flown there will be
other surprises: the cleanliness
of their stalls, the secret cache of books,
diaries in which they recorded
fine gradations of emotion.

II.

Book of Hours

Yourself
and light, being both mortal, have much
in common.

       ***

In the sky tumbling overhead
threaded on stars
you encounter another emptiness,
that is not yours.

       ***

Evening
leant too far from the top-floor window
and fell.

       ***

Now the sky puts on its hat
and at last it is dark.
The same darkness grows
in doors and cabinets,
at the back of your throat.

       ***

Open your eyes,
release the morning.

What the Days Bring

not gold or silver
but paper

paper like flesh
impermanent, a makeshift container
because it's what we have

like playing Beethoven on banjo

clouds were low on the mountains
the sun not far behind

that she said is our life
and tapped at the window pane

Late News

Your paintings will climb down
off the wall and attack me.
I cannot escape them. The world
is weather and misunderstanding.

One wants to go back, to the old
ways, a house with green walls,
shelves, but your feet
are always somewhere else,

waiting for you to catch up,
moving away from all those
memories, boxes within boxes
there in the corners of the night,

stacked, tottering.

Watching the Clock

when you sense the day
extending its hand to you

and yellow candles go on inventing darkness

when
the luggage of morning flies open
releasing
the sun which has not slept well

and birds drag blue across the sky

when she who is your other self
turns to the wall
dreaming tomorrow into place
the window's eye unblinking

the bones stand up out of you
restless
you hear them moving about
in the next room

Sheridan Square

    (for Tom Disch)

Empty

Room   sky   hand
and that voice at the door   knocking

Locked in this room   I see people in command of windows
The noise of the city
congeals like mud on their shoes
Gray pigeons wheel up and scatter into blue-green sky
where it's summer

How many times I think
have I turned back   hand
on that door   thoughts crowding behind me on the platform
Turn the handle   the tongue falls like a latch
Compartments open

Now here I am on foot among scattered bags
Taxis ride the plains   I whistle at one to bring it down
Here on the frontier   Muleskinner and sage
A birch rod dips
toward sacred words   Everything's out of tune Tom

Water?   Rain at least
And me with this dwarf's crutch I'm trying to sell
There's little demand   Pawnshops and women turn me out
here where it's summer
here where everything's out of tune

here where I've tried   *j'ai fait*
des gestes blancs parmi les solitudes
Taking out ads in The Voice
Renting billboards   Light of the day squinting

from under the bushel of years

Urging them all
just to stop   but they go on turning

hand   sun   year   room   self

June 6th

At 11:01 I listen to Brahms,
drink tea, and wait
to hear from you.

Wellington's Victory ends
at a minute to twelve.
Driving through city lights

and limits, I thought of you
asleep, the long white beach
of your back, dreams

like malformed moons
in whatever sky
vaults above you now.

All battles join at night.
A spider
parachutes onto my desk

from the lamp
and charges across,
the first wave of freedom.

Return

And I have come from
Bright edges
To be here   I have come from pills
And drops locked tight
In the chambers

From the voice
Of razors
And the secret syllables of gas

Who called me back

I have come
Without words
Into this leap of days in array
The crowd lugs up behind me
Like an old beach

I have come from mistakes
Lodged in the corners of eyes I have come back
From blood

In May

Your pain and my desire
in the rain tonight, this rain
that insists
I build a house of intention
to live in.

Air catches in our lungs
like sparks
as water against the window
presses
the world into place.

Light tiptoes across the floor
trailing gray
regrets. Pushing at the
rain's hands,
walls pop and moan.

III.

The Sisters of Sheldon Street

The old women waiting for cataclysm
open their doors to no one. Even they
have misplaced their names now: two I's,
the ring of needs around them
grown ever smaller, wants expired.

Morning sketches the outlines
of trees then fills them in as one lies dreaming
she will wed a skeleton
whose bones are whiter than her lace gown.

Wind at the door again as they wait
for water, ice, storm, something
that will consume them.
From the well of their days, buckets
come up, as empty as Father's heart.

When they die, others will discover
among their things, twin diaries
bound in leather, hand-stitched,
in which no entries have been made.

Spy Story

(for Mike Moorcock)

The street is still.
He sits watching the leaf of a fern,
that never moves. (—Your passport,
Mr. Cornelius? —Which one?) *The first colony
was established in June, 1971,
in Boston. Initial reports were ambiguous.
How to penetrate their defenses?*

A child stands beside him. As he ages,
so does the child.
The two cannot easily be told apart now. (—There
would appear to be some confusion,
Mr. Cornelius.) *The social order
uncertain, there appeared men
who had no society. Only guilt or faith,
that they fed. A woman might be the answer.*

(He slept poorly. The years were there.
At three she waked him, said Love me.
Thoughts of other men, she had told them
how he was; other cities, other reasons.
The next morning
she was sick. She called to tell him that.
He heard her at four in the bathroom. He slept.
Good-bye he said as the plane slipped into Boston clouds.)

*The expedition was recalled.
There had been no positive result.
Another would be dispatched, with a complement
of scholars.*

Of the Voyage

Listen. There's little time left and
the trees grow smaller, the flowers
every day more deadly.

I've seen the other side,
been to the other side,
and madness sits there, resplendent.

His teeth are beads
rattling at the window.
His tongue dives and rolls in the depths
of his mouth like a whale.

Beyond the window,
ships fall away from port
like chips from flint.
They throw no shadows on the water.

Listen: the wind makes no sound. Look:
In this kingdom always
there is something walking beside the day
besides the day.

Speechless

The glove has died there alongside
the vase. A left-hand glove, pink,
and the vase yet contains
the remains of five blue flowers
in an inch of sewery water.

The world, he thinks, is a single long word,
broken to segments when the gods stutter.

Wind whispers
through a crack beneath the door:
Come out, come out.
Rain waits
to be called onstage.

Victory

Later that glorious, fateful day, after
beakers of raw alcohol and bitter coffee
in our camp behind the churchyard, we gathered
for a march down the only street they had.
Those left alive, children, bent old women
and frail, trembling men, sundered wives,
stood watching. They cheered. Their cheers
were hollow, empty, like their faces.
Whatever they had is ours now.

Saviors

In the withering garden I sat
beside the man who had brought
down a regime
with the weight of his words.

A breeze stepped gingerly
in the grass—as though the very trees
breathe for us, he said.

In memory of privations his people
underwent, he had not bathed or eaten
for some time. Knees and narrow legs
stuck up from his chair like a grasshopper's.

Any moment I might hear the sound of wings.

Gauge

    (for Boris Vian)

I'm so tired of it, the women with trees
Between their legs, the forest of possible eductions.
And the stork riding its ridiculous red roses
Towards us across the desert
Again.

                        the tracks progressing well
                        cable, Ready soon, rails laid on time
                        the locomotive will

Red needles swing across the face of our days, leaving red
Behind. Mensurate, commiserate. Anacoluthon—hearing
Delicious lips open inside a morning. The giraffe's snakelike
Heads silent above the trees.

                        commensurate, comminution, commisure

And the silver threads dashing along cobalt seams,
Day. The comity of nations continues, allows us to remain
Here. Horizons appear at intervals. Then the work stops;
An ostrich comes to borrow water from our tanks.

                        and other manifestations of length, duration
                        the absence of ants, flies, inchworms
                        the moths crouched waiting

Insects desert the sun in a line from the horizon, in single
File. Gracchus laughs and watches each queue and wait
Its turn. He names them. Another cable, Rails almost done
Trees down No more Please cable return Further
Instructions

                        horizons vanish

Feet among ties, even the giraffes are waiting. We release
The construction into the landscape. It scatters,
Correcting the sand's pronunciation; it lies under the sun
In articulate fragments, random as facts. Someone applauds.

                        "there was no other choice"
                        "but within lie other choices"
                        the cable unanswered

The insects pause, then march one by one into the aardvark's
Dead mouth—and tumble
In knots from the eyes. We wait, and watch.

Stand-Up

    (for Fred Chappell)

here comes death
with a new joke

never tells them right
gets the details wrong
screws up the punch lines
timing sucks

now that's *funny*
death says
having botched it

"a priest a rabbi
and an undertaker
go into this bar"

gonna be a long day

Badges

1.

They circle in their white clothes
around the table where he lies
much as he lay on your bed, his head
now a red pineapple.
There is no sense in this; no reason.
Clothes are cut off, discarded,
his shield a bright eye among them.
The sough of pumps, the tick of tiny engines
is to you familiar ground
above which the sky has changed irrevocably.

2.

The wind off the hall is so chill.
You shiver in the office chair. Memories
crowd around you and you cannot breathe.
You cannot understand. This
is what we all fear: the face turning slowly
towards us becoming one we know.
You wear a white coat. You walk stiff-kneed,
heavy. Your body will not support you.
Your name, what you are,
hangs like a bullet over your heart.

Water

Each morning at ten the old men
meet in the park
to start up again
their game of old lives.

Billy wins the election,
Doug's been in love
with the same woman
for forty years, Doc never shot
that kid in Korea.

Cooled by the shadows
of their imaginings,
the old men sit in the heat.

Long afternoon lies on its side
like an abandoned shoe,
empty, empty.

Artaud

The revolt against poetry
continues. No more literature!
And yet, language goes on working
its way up out of you, through you.

What you know, you will know
absolutely, you insist—or not at all.
Metaphors bring to mind
those floppy rubber boots the British wear.

Tears down all walls!
Bury all towers!

Then you pause and we see
in your eyes what you know:
you are yourself the world
you demolish, the only world.

For Queneau

The judge's black robes
are like a crow's.

Outside his window an oak tree
grows silently
so as not to disturb the judge's thoughts.

Children swarm in bright rooms
as a woman prepares dinner. Her gas stove
lisps in the twilight.

Tottering on the branches of the oak,
the sky takes a deep breath
and closes its eyes.

The judge's hand moves across the page,
 leaving the spoor of letters,
 of his dissension, behind.

He lifts an apricot to the mouth
where his death waits.

New Life

This time he has gone
too far, lurching

from the bed at 4 AM.
The sink fills

with blood and thin
clear fluid (he has not eaten

today), What
has he done.

Beer and scotch, a discussion
of religious experience

with a linguist that he
can't remember. The world

vanished at 8 PM; still,
he moved

through it. Watch:
he walks

on the edge of razors. Blood
runs down them, ruins

them, the edge. Maybe
that.

Scat Singers

On the last day of her life, Becky walked about the house from room to room with a small music box, winding and playing it repeatedly. She'd bought it years ago in Sedona, on a trip with visiting friends, for $7.95; it played "Flight of the Bumblebee." She remembered the red rocks that day. Just before the end, she began to hum along.

On the last day of his life, José sat on the patio he'd never finished, five or six years now since he started, its railings and floorboards bare, the bench alive with splinters. Memories crouched in his mind like hawks on tree limbs. Fine intentions whisper inside your head, he thought, fine intentions that are never a match for the noise outside.

On the last day of his life, Hannes packed his guitar for the gig and sat waiting for dark and the reduced prices at the diner up the street. Half asleep in the chair, he had a dream. He was playing somewhere, a trio with bass and piano, and there was a rest. He knew he had to come in soon, but he couldn't remember: Two bars? Four and a half?

Ars Poetica

They are all in possession, she said,
of this splinter of wood they believe
may become a tree again.

If you'll wait a moment, she said,
I can get one for you. I paid—
well, never mind, it was worth
every penny, though.

Politely I asked what she might
do with it. I don't know, she said,
whatever magic was in there is gone
or used up, it won't work for me.

It *is* so beautiful though, she said,
in the morning when light
catches it just so.

Stalking the Wild MFA

"It's all about getting the lie right," Morton Graves says. He holds his coffee mug in both hands and sips meaningfully away. God knows what's in there.

Man, we aren't here for this Zen shit. We want to hear about agents, movie sales and book signings, what publisher or small press will look at our shit. Like that. Practical stuff. Tips from a pro.

The woman with the purple hair and tights has published 109 *vignettes* and *feuilletons* in online magazines, not to mention her daily blog, now at #562. Each morning her mailbox is filled with messages from *followers*.

The guy who looks like he's fourteen complete with backpack for his books has interest from an editor at Thor House. Another three, four, maybe six months and the blessed thing'll be on its way. He's brought in his sketches for flyers and action figures to show us.

A memoir, the new one says (that word alone enough to strike terror into all our hearts), seen through the lens of the future. Yes, the future. And he has been at this, beating away at his wee soundless drum, for fourteen years.

"You are in a dark room," Morton Graves tells us, "and someone is whispering—in a language you don't understand.

"*Listen*," he says, and a hush comes in, sits down beside us.

Screen Doors

Turning back he thinks "But I meant—"
What *was* it he meant or intended?
To do, to say.

How she will stand watching
through the screen door,
and the flapping of sheets on the line.

Day bends over the bag it packs to leave,
saying "I understand"

as another world prepares
to empty itself of him.

Baroque

"Could I place
my love in plastic
cubes, tubes, you

would have
shelves full—shelves full
and a case

of crystal glass
to keep them in.

Against the wall's
flowers in thin clear fluids

that catch the
sun, it would float like
tonsils, tumors,

and other things taken from me."

IV.
NEW SURREALIST POEMS

The Surrealist Comes to Black Rock

When he stepped off the train,
silverware clattered in drawers
all over town. Children knew
to stay indoors.
Women and businessmen
broke out their best clothes
waiting for bells to ring.

The Surrealist Travels by Train

Alone at night his hands
swing the red lanterns
slowly out, he looks about
for terrible wasps he will not hear.

The Girl the Surrealist Left Behind

There beneath the rock
that sunlight holds
in the dark hollow of its hand
she crouches. Earth, she knows,
would have its fingers in her.
Shivering, too, whenever someone
breathes the word *sea*.

The Surrealist Relocates

Where he has come to settle,
in this language, her language,
the poem is a river.

Here one cannot say *I want, I long for*,
he writes in a letter back home.
One says instead "The river leaves at ten,"

"This day will be beautiful in the river,"
or (once she leaves)
"The river empties into her eyes."

The Plan Behind Improvisation

The surrealist lies awake listening to fish in the walls.
He collects them, has for years, and needs only the blue-fin
to fill that space on his shelf.
Unique among fish, the blue-fin sings.
This is the last one, he knows; they've never been recorded.
Still, it will look so fine up there, alongside
Mailer, Kerouac and a stack of fresh towels,
morning light like a passing thought glinting off its scales.

Surrealist Bird

Though the eggs are long gone (stolen
by bluejays, sucked dry, shelved away
on high branches), surrealist bird
still sits her nest of words.

Something will hatch.

Surrealist bird makes her way, gliding,
among the city's canyons
and spires, throws down the anchor
of a single, sharp cry.

Something will die.

Sky peels away in shreds
as surrealist bird flies, ever careful
to move away from those bare patches,
those doorways, those invitations.

The Surrealist Prays

To the Great Masturbator, whose seed
becomes world, heaven,
all between and beneath

To the Great Nose, who sneezed
existence, all that is,
into Being

To the Great Anesthetist who,
our pain become too great at last,
finds mercy for us
in His own impure heart

Surrealist on the Move

The surrealist walks through the town.
Above his head, on statues,
riders leap from their horses.

The surrealist has coffee at a small café.
Flowers cover the tabletop
as he lifts his cup.

All about him, women sit stiffly upright,
in each of their eyes
a single tear that never falls.

The Surrealist Remembers His Friend

You wrote of the mouths
of wind, of day
like a suckling child
at sun's breast.

At night those mouths
came again
and your name
was inside them.

V.

Done

When tomorrow you come begging
he will not know you.

Whatever you find to say, he
will not hear. Radios that played your songs
will remain silent as knobs are turned
and turned again.

Lights will dim as you walk past houses.

Loss

1.

Now the day floats on the pond.
The sky choked in promise.

Silence closes around itself.

2.

Within itself the day revolves
and returns
to where I stand

At this bright yellow edge

Accompanied by the sound,
borne on the level backs,
of hornets.

3.

Lost in interior gardens—
on the inside of flowers, alone.

Following the prints of the fly's hooves.

A life
led only to this.

Seasons

1.

Sinking in the slough of self
he throws out a hand: wolves devour it.
He scrabbles for purchase
with his feet: fish swallow them.

Stockstill in evening light
he is alone. He revolves from purpose
to pleasure, admitting himself

piecemeal to the sky.

2.

When she goes, he finds
a word for that. When she returns,
that will be another word.

Phrases live on, live on air, in the false
bottoms of trunks. Tongues
wrap about hard facts and stick.

Sentences falter. Memories fail.
The world rusts into winter.

Family

       (Sagittarius)

That wounded archer let go
Past midnight
The arrow struck   I
Was the place my mother landed

Half man half other

       (Cancer)

The red warmth of that other world
Massive inside me
I feel the sting   Already
You are scuttling away

So small in the sand

       (Capricorn)

Gored
You move that horned leg
They lean close
There is the sound   then

Your feet clattering down hospital
Halls

Fall

Woods
from which the beast peers
smiling

We see its bright eyes there
Sunlight's cinders

Night
with its dark flag
of surrender

Some Propositions

I am not
yours, etc.

I don't know
should you stay
or go, I
hardly know you

And I have seen
to the darkness under
it all, etc.

And I have accepted
the darkness under it
all, etc.

In this world

Final Landscape

The hooves
of the sea

At the edge
of the forest
watching

    ***

On the slope there

Hands
turning in air

Where you open
voices

    ***

The rocks
from which you step

And the sound of the sky

Christmas 1969

So many dead men
Under the snow to think

What are their feet doing now
Without them

       ***

Eyes roll slowly through the snow
Tracks like treadless tires
Every few moments
Black spots appear

       ***

Hands white
On the tree with other limbs
Far off they understand their loss
We hear their cries

VI.

Compass

The desk where I work faces east,
and when I'm putting in
long hours, reaching for the end of a book
or clutching at the straw that might
end a piece perfectly,
moss sprouts on my left side.

It's as though a warm quilt found its way
to my face and arm and leg.
As though my body has become two halves.
As though north decided to befriend me.

 But can I trust what it tells me?
Comforting, protective, the moss
glints like fool's gold
where light from the desklamp hits it.
It matches the clockwork of my socks.

In my hour of need it's come,
to give direction.

Last Call

1.

Hours after the blast
and I know I'm the only one
left alive,

I unlock the door
and begin to make decisions,
bring in the trash
that will never be picked up.

2.

The server brings the muffin and says
You have to hurry, the world
shuts down in six minutes.

She has to go, she says.
Enjoy.

Her boyfriend in a green raincoat
waves come here,
waves good-bye,
through the glass.

3.

I've seen this so many times
(the barkeep says of the sitcom
in the TV floating above her head)
that every one of them has swapped partners
twice now. There's nothing left.

Then one of them up there kills someone
and genre is born.

Once Upon Again

And will I see you, then, on the edge
of evening

Body poised at the door jamb,
hand stuck in time between pressure
and buzzer's sting

Square after square
on these walls, above the floor
of a studio once the color of limes

Sticking as usual, the door opens
while paintings on the wall behind urge:
Look up here, you fool!

And you look at me

The Surrealist Is Interviewed on 60 Minutes

In Neuville we do not order pizza
when company comes over.
There are no checkbooks, and insects
don't care for the way we taste.

When hard wind arrives, it only wants
to tell us what it's been reading,
or to pose complex riddles;
it speaks in whispers.

Soon enough Monday will give way
to Tuesday, and again we must paint the houses gray,
hang kitchen utensils from the trees.

Hello, Citizen! We all will cry from the tops
of our ladders. Speaking for the children,
speaking to the sullen crows.

Lost Letters

My mail man is not a happy man.
Life, he thinks, has dealt him a bad hand,
a bad deal so to say, and you feel it in the way
his own hand deals mail

through the slot in my front door,
as though in yet another game
he knows he has no chance of winning.

I watch him make his way down the street,
legs growing shorter between houses,
taking him inch by inch, year by year,
ever closer, grumbling, to the ground.

When I Had the Sky

When I could fly
such things bothered me little:
the lack of party invitations, that
I had no new shoes for school,
or the way Jimmy put gum in my hair
every Friday.

I knew when the bell rang
the sky
would be waiting for me outside.

Stars would wince like cats
and the town below me be transformed
to nothing more
than a spread of doll houses for sale,
models, imagined things.

Nothing
to do with me.

As We Were

Here, we do not change.

Shaking heads, we watch
new worlds
taking form outside
our windows, our screens.

We cannot understand.

This sort of thing could
come here, move in, catch on.

We go on watching
as light borrows another night,
saying
it will pay us back.

Resolve

Today I am throwing out (she said)
all the unread telegrams of the heart.
I must make room.
It's got so we can barely walk
in here for tripping over them.

They sputtered in
one after another, eight or ten
at a time some days. In bunches,
like bags of walnuts, or bananas.
And what can you do with these things?

They're all the same
once you open them: O the hurt,
I'm so lonely, Might you consider…?
Or memories that won't hold together
however much glue you use.

Tomorrow and your life
are a one-legged child
crossing towards you behind the door.
You hear the footfall, wait
for the next. And wait.

Fortune

    (for Amy)

Here I sit, drawing false maps
of how we met, doing my best
to stay inside the lines. Here's a memory
of your hand moving towards my face,
there the curve of the city
carressing a river that won't let go.

Memories of your parents are burned
onto the walls of the house
where you still live. Your brother,
who never came home from a vacation
you later learned was Afghanistan. The doll
who when you were ten stopped talking to you.

Behind us a smudge of horizon where the sun
went down, somewhere in the house
the sound of your aloneness
banging at headboards, nothing but silence
from the back room where you keep bags packed,
three of them, for alternative futures.

www.ingramcontent.com/pod-product-compliance
Lightning Source LLC
Chambersburg PA
CBHW071749080526
44588CB00013B/2198